SO
YOUNG
YET
SO
HIGH

SO YOUNG YET SO HIGH

GWEN LEROUY

SO YOUNG YET SO HIGH

iUniverse books may be ordered through booksellers or by contacting:

iUniverse
1663 Liberty Drive
Bloomington, IN 47403
www.iuniverse.com
1-800-Authors (1-800-288-4677)

ISBN: 978-1-5320-4012-2 (sc)
ISBN: 978-1-5320-4013-9 (e)

Print information available on the last page.

iUniverse rev. date: 01/23/2018

I will start with telling you some of my childhood. Not all but some…I was born and raised in mn. I've lived here most of my life. I am the youngest of four. Dan, Devon,and Sammy are my syblings. My parents stayed married all the way up to my father's passing. My parents are alcoholics and partied a lot during my childhood. My father was a veteran with bi-polar disorder, PTSD. He struggled threw out his life to stay stable and sober. He always worked hard. Then he became 100% disabled vet due to a accident during his time in battle. My mom was a stylist, then stayed at home with us kids. She was wonderful. Both my parents are. They just faught a lot during his manic times and alcohol use. I can remember several times my father got violent and the police had to come. My father would put his hands on my mom a lot in front of us. He's done many things to her in front of us. He had lots of DWI's and was unstable most of his life. I hated him because of what he all did to her. Later learning and understanding his mental health and alcoholism is why he did what he did. It was hard growing up in this household. My mom kept us together always and did everything for everyone else. She never was able to take care of anything for herself. She had to take care of my dad, and us. She's a wonderful strong woman. I am the youngest of four and my siblings and I to this day aren't very close due to what we all went threw during or childhood. I wish we where but we are not. My family today does't call one another we are distant and when we do hang out it usually used to involve alcohol, or drugs. Not so mch now that we are older. I struggled as a child always felt left out, the youngest not smart enough, and always was left behind with the siblings because of the age difference.

All my syblings where moved out my parents partied the night before. My father was drinking again but sneaking his Yukon Jack downstairs. My mom was hungover and she was always mean whenever she was hung over. I went downstairs and caught my dad sneaking his alcohol. I told him mom knew, but instead went upstairs and told my mom what he had been doing. She got all crazy screaming at the top of her lungs…"Quit your drinking"! You DRUNK! He came upstairs and started choking her right in front of me. I started screaming and crying o the top of my lungs!! STOP, STOP!! Of course he didn't. So I grabbed him by his throat from behind and kicked him in the back of his knees. Him then falling to his knees. I was scared to death but I had to save mom as always. She had a way about her mouth that always got us into trouble. He turned and looked at me, and I was in tears scared to death. Please god I prayed have this stop…. And he did he then seen the fear and how scared I was he went to the back room. Mom was in shock at what had just happened. The next we acted as though it never happened. That's what we had always done. Things never changed all the trauma we went threw mom would never leave him. I can remember saying to my mom if he hits you one more time, will you leave him. She said yes. I can remember praying this one session or fight my parents had that he would hit her so she would then leave him. Of course he did hit her but she never left. The next day it would be as if nothing ever happened. Being the youngest of four we all mimic what our syblings do. My two older brothers got into the dope game. MY second oldest brother sold lots of cocaine, and my other brother was a chronic addict like myself. I seen my oldest brother pistol whip my second oldest brother. He also robbed him a few times. I never witnessed that but only imagined how bad that was. I was braught up into this life. I didn't know any different. Party is what you did to have fun since that's all I really seen growing up. We did have some good memories but they are all a blurr today. My parents did the best they could with what they had. This is just a piece of what we all went threw growing up and how it was. Growing up I never was braught up to know God, and I never believed in him. I had no chance really I was lost from the very beginning.

My Life here ...In Prison I remember the day I was on my way back to prison, February 14ᵗʰ 2010! What a wonderful Valentine's day...so I thought. Looking back today, it was the unfailing love of God, giving me another chance with his patience and grace at life.

See, I've already been to prison once, did 2 years from 2008-2010; today it is 2011. I sat those years here in Prison listening to Satin's lies...I did break out of his bondage of "I don't deserve to be loved or be happy"

Today I am Free, and happy.

After I was released from prison on June 17ᵗʰ 2010; see it was actually a shock. I remember walking out not believing or comprehending that I could actually get in the car and go, and never go back. Or so I thought.

That day I went to my parents house. My dad came and picked me up, smoking like he always has one after another,

At this time, I was not close to God at all. I had pushed him away the beginning of my stay in my time served at Prison.

I got released from the Work Release Program on June 17ᵗʰ 2010.

During my stay in the work release program through prison, I was already drinking a beer here and there. I was also sneaking over to the father of my child's house. Even though I knew I had no intentions of being with him. I knew I did not love him at all. I always had a guy. I also had a guy I was writing getting out of prison I wanted to meet up with, who later I almost used Meth with. I also had my ex Sam who wanted to be with me.

I just wanted what I wanted from them...Honestly was pretty much done with men because of what I had been through. They were nothing to me. They've done nothing but abused me, physically, mentally, verbally, and emotionally.. I will get into more details later..

Backing up to my first time I came to prison.. See, I had been with a girl before I came to Prison. I thought men had done nothing but hurt me, so maybe a women could love me. I felt appreciated, and taken care of, a sense of comfort from her.

See, we were in a Christian based treatment program together. I thought of her as my close friend who I thought was very beautiful. I actually remember being a bit jealous of her at first. I knew she was a lesbian, she had no shame in her game, I actually was attracted to her confidence, love, independence, and the love she showed me even though- I'd push her away..because of my discontentment, Now remember this is before I was sentenced 36 months in prison. We did everything together; read the bible, had coffee together, wrestle read, work-out, smoke cigs, and gossip, and plan evil plans together. See, when I got there I came right from jail from a prior parole violation/ my house arrest.

See she was doing really good on her walk with God. Looking back now I corrupted her and Satan worked through me to draw her back into his strong hold of bondage through meth addiction.

But threw my lost soul and her sexual desires, and by curiosity of bi-sexual, and being hurt by men so much, we gave into Satan's temptations.

We made love for the 1st time..It was very awkward, even though-in the past...I had 3somes and kissed a girl...never had sexual relations with one. I did not go down on her...After that our friendship became on a different level...I still was attracted to men, and we came to the conclusion there was "no strings attached", mainly because I was unsure about the situation or what had happened. I know I had feelings for her, But didn't know what exactly they were.

At this time I was waiting to be sentenced on my 2nd and 3rd degree sales. Which I already had 3 felony points prior, and was on probation when I was charged with these charges.

Throughout the years of my path of destruction, and worshipping the devil as my father...I would pray the "dear god, I need your help" when I was in jail, desperate with a spirit of fear, pain no self worth, and brokenness that was undesirable...

See, Jesus was always there, reaching out to me, trying to grab my hand... I only would pray when I was in the depths of HELL, or so I thought,,, Here really it was God saving me from Satan's strong holds.

I am the one who has seen the afflictions that came from the rod of the lords anger.

I'd pray in desperation...God! If you please... Get me out of this one...Usually when I was in jail coming down off of the Devils' Dandruff which is meth. I'd make promises to God, get out and wonder off his path. Back on to the road of addiction, and hell of destruction. See each time gets worse when you go back.

Here I sit in Prison ... writing this to you as a message from god., who is working threw me to have you see the love, light, and beautiful plan he has for your life. Just ask him to open your eyes to see.

I remember sitting in jails, sleeping for days...God still there with his love, patience and grace...Watching over me healing my soul. That maybe I would open my heart to him.

Satan knows our weaknesses, and has been prowling around watching us as a fallen angel, even when we were children, he was there...trying to test us. ..he puts evil thoughts, feelings, desires, evil plans, strong holds on us through our minds, to keep us away from god and to spiritually drawn our soul. Then we are worshipping him, Satan as our God.

In the blood of Jesus I pray... Rebuke Satan through your mind, thoughts, and spirit. Hold every evil thought capture, and identify which is from Satan or from god.

Lets back up a little bit. I was at the Christian based program in sexual sin the first time with a female...this is where Satan got to the both of us. I basically said "I knew I was coming to prison..I just couldn't deal with that and became upset, with god about his will, for me was to come to Prison. This is where I rebelled against god, gave up.,, on myself, My faith, and just wanted to ease my pain...Of course than Satan knew my soul. I guess you could say my companion at the time, Satan worked through me and her weakness of her sexual desires, my looks, That time I was deceitful, and corrupted with Satan's' strong holds.

I continued our relationship between her and I...leading her to the path of Satan's road of destruction for the both of us...

We kept on with our sexual sin between her and I ...I got to get out of the faith based program to go to aftercare treatment. So I would get to get smokes, secular music, cuz the faith based program was extremely strict we couldn't go anywhere without staff. One day after treatment I thought this guy was beautiful. I had seen him at a meeting. I could see he felt the same about me, so we started talking on the phone. I couldn't get out of the faith based program. He was doing good at the time, and I was extremely attracted to him. The only thing that was bad was that I knew I was coming to prison. So really, I didn't want any man at all...I just wanted to run as far away from my prison sentence as I could.

Now the relationship between her and I, I was still unsure about. She could tell, she really wanted to be with me. I was and still am attracted more to men then to women. This is a sin God and I are still working on within me. So, I could tell that when I would be talking to him on the phone she was jealous, or hurt... but I had told her from the beginning "no strings attached" Even though to this day I still have a place in my heart for her. She was the first female I experienced this with.

Anyways- so, I kept talking to him on the phone, and she still wanted me...I honestly didn't care because I was going to Prison. So he started to use meth. I continued to go to my aftercare treatment, And that way I would get a chance to go sneak off and meet up with him. It was summertime... him and I have been talking and he wanted us to be together...I didn't know what I wanted. I knew I really liked him, and liked her. But I knew I couldn't deal with being with anyone when I was locked up. I tried to explain this to him. Plus, at this time men didn't' mean nothing to me..They've done nothing but hurt me. So that's why I was with her as well. Satan had me so hurt in so many ways at this time, I trusted no one, sometimes not even myself. Being at this Christian based program the faith based program. brought me back to Jesus for a minute, but after I found out I was going to go to prison, and not be able to stay there, instead, I said "F it" and gave up!

Back to when I snuck from my aftercare treatment to meet up with him. When I saw him, he was on meth. I could see it in his eyes. Instantly I had a trigger. I wanted it so bad... We talked and we were down by the river just talking... about us, and how he was so into me.la, la, la!! Heard that so many times, never again would I put my heart out there for anyone ever again.

Yes, I can say I had feelings for him, but not as much as he did. I was extremely attracted to him so I wanted to just have him, and I knew he wanted me too. So, I just got what I wanted or what we both wanted. We had sexual relations down by the river, and he also hooked me up with the devil's dandruff. which is meth. So again Satan got to me working through him, and his beauty, my sexual desires toward him, and my fear upon my prison sentence.

So, when I say Satan works threw people to get to us with our weaknesses.. He uses the people with lost souls who are his (Satan's), which the souls that belong to Satan are the dark powers of the unseen world, or evil spirits...

After He and I had our little love session.... Or so he thought...I just got what I wanted. I was high, got my needs met, and got more for my girl at the Christian place.

See I was a lost soul as well, God had never given up on me, I always given up on him... I knew I needed to get as high as I could cuz I was eventually going to prison for years.

So, I got back

I was still on parole and was court ordered to be at the faith based program., and had to follow all rules and regulations.

I never once did that.. I don't recall a treatment or a place I've been locked up that would honestly follow all rules. That's probably one of the many reasons god has me in his love and care here in Prison.

I was high, paranoid, my soul was under Satan's complete control;. I had given up on God, knew I was on my way to prison...

And new soon enough I was out of this place.

So, her and I got together in her room... she could tell I was high, she was sober, until later... But we too had relations, and she showed me how.

After that we did some lines of the devils dandruff. We both became his. So Satan worked through me to get her to try meth for her first time, and worked threw her to give in to my female sexuality.

The next day we were both coming down I remember going to the chapel high on crystal meth, feeling gods conviction deep within my heart. I was extremely ashamed to be in his presence.

See god speaks to us threw his words (the bible), threw people (true Christians, pastors, ministers, etc.) and our consciences. Our intuition, the feeling that we get when we know we are doing something wrong but we do it anyway. Our sin.

Once you were dead because of your disobedience and your many sins. you used to live in sin, just like the rest of the world, obeying the-the commander of the powers of the unseen world. He is the spirit at work in our hearts of those who refuse to obey god. Ephesians 2:1-s

That was me, Satan's spirit was at work in my heart completely. I am writing this to you through the gift of the holy spirit from god, it is god who is using me to glorify him, and to reach out to the addicts who Satan has control over. I know and understand what you're experiencing with your meth addiction.

So, backing up to being high on crystal meth (Devil's Dandruff) in the chapel feeling convicted in the presence of god.

See, I only knew or became saved through jails... I never knew him growing up...All that I knew in my knowledge was I knew for a fact I wasn't supposed to be praising God high on meth...

So, after programming, we thought, planned of ways to get out and get more meth.

See, there we should not even go outside...unless we were taking out the garbage. So, of course I called up him..who I had feelings for and knew I could get him to basically do whatever I wanted him to do...He was aware of all the rules there at faith based program. anyways.

We planned to take out the garbage, and him just as a coincidence... happen to drive by, as we were bringing the garbage out. I waved at him, and went up to his vehicle and he put the bag in my hand. Then I walked away from his vehicle back to where she was by the dumpster dumping the garbage. As I continued to help her with the garbage. By this time both her and I were coming down hard core. So, I had to hook-up...Of course we got questioned because there is eyes and ears everywhere around the faith based program. there all Christians that live in and around the building.

So, we got the meth in there, and we got all spun out. Then later that night I came up with this bright idea, that we needed more dope. and was talking to him on the phone. I wanted to meet up with him. So we ended up sneaking out...of the faith based program. I could tell she was very uncomfortable, but really at that time my heart, mind, and soul was completely gone...So, I didn't care about anyone or anything...all I cared about was easing the pain I've felt inside for so long, and my prison sentence...thoughts...which I wanted to completely avoid at all costs completely and meth was my way to deal.

So both she and I snuck out of the faith based program. met up with him, went out to this house, got all high, then came back. we never got caught..which was pretty unbelievable.

God knows everything I have done he has always been right there... although I always thought I could hide or avoid him completely.

See, I was saved October 18th of 2007 at the jail, I asked the lord to come into my heart. I continued to seek him (read his word) grew strong in my faith but continued to drift off his path.. due to Satan's temptations working threw people, places, and things. I would always thought I could ignore, avoid, or run from god. He is always watching both the good and the evil.

god is always watching no matter where we are...no matter where we are...God has seen all that I have done...Brought meth into a Christian based program (the faith based program.), I had given upon praying, praising, and had corrupchuck her, not to mention another women that was also in the program. Gave up completely on god, mainly because I had been praying I could stay at the faith based program. instead of going to prison. God had said no.

See, god works through everyone, and everything for the good. His plan was different than what I had in mind. So I was angry with god..

Especially having to go through all the trials and tribulations that I experienced before I knew him. I was still scarred, and continued to run from that as well.

I was sad spiritually broken inside, and no one could fill my heart where I felt incomplete, and certainly not god either. or any significant other. The only thing that could help me was the devils dandruff... Satan got me back into his trap, and back down the road of destruction...

I remember feeling my soul being completely taken over like so many times throughout my addiction.. not knowing what was going on spiritually... I gave my soul to Satan once again...

Stay alert watch out for your great enemy, the devil, he prowls around like a roaring lion, looking for someone to devour.. Stand firm against him and be strong in your faith...

Peter 3:

I didn't know what to do with myself... I was the devils for so long, I felt comfort giving up on myself and staying far from god. I could not overcome my sin.. I still loved god, Just couldn't live by him... I was struggling with wanting to live for him at this time, but also wanting the pain, heartache, abuse that I went through to go away...

Romans 7:14

Struggling with sin
So the trouble is not with the law for it is spiritual and good. The trouble is with me for I am all too human, a slave to sin. I don't really understand myself, for I want to do what is right, but I don't do it. Instead I do what I hate. But if I know that what I am doing is wrong, this shows that I agree that the law is good. roman 7:14-16

I didn't want to feel, live or hurt anymore... I hated myself for failing in everything I would do... I gave up on myself completely, I wanted to numb, and party my life away. I knew I was coming to prison... So, I went back to selling my soul once again to Satan.

For I envied the proud... when I saw them prosper despite their wickedness, they seemed to live such painless lives; their bodies are so healthy and strong. they don't have trouble like other people, they're not plagued with problems like everyone else. Psalm 73=3-6

So I continued on the road back onto destruction.

I ended up getting a dirty UA, kicked out of the program at faith based program., both her and I left the treatment. I was then on the run, and waiting for my sentencing court date.

My family once again was going through hell right along with me... I've broken my mother's heart so many times throughout my life... I still have guilt and shame to this day about how many times I've hurt her...

My siblings had just straight up given up after my house got raided, and god put a stop to my selling drugs. I'll tell you about the morning my house got raided.

I remember the night before my place got raided (my co-defendant) and myself were trippin on acid or LSD, we had been selling large amounts of meth, ecstasy, and had been using mushrooms, and acid for our pleasure.

He and I had been up for days selling, partying, committing all kinds of crimes... first off selling, using, transporting drugs, boosting (stealing) merchandise from places, collecting money, that was owed to us... having hearts of stones... See him and myself were partners in crime, we spent a lot of time together committing lots of crimes. I've known him since 5th grade. Went to junior high with his younger sister... so we were riders, and we went good together... we weren't a couple... although he would compare us to Bonnie and Clyde... He wanted us to be connected. I just felt, and knew that he was more like my bro, and yes I did have feelings for him... Yet I wasn't physically attracted to him.

Okay so back to the night before my house got raided. Both of us had been extremely busy doing our business...Here, There, everywhere...See he had fallen out, and when I say he was falling out.. this means passed out... we had moved all the dope that we had received, accept a couple of 8 balls of dope... which we were about to go and re-up that morning, thank god we didn't...

So, the night before my house got raided I remember having all these satanic evil thoughts... thoughts of suicide, wanting to just off myself... I couldn't go another day living my life I was living... I hated myself and wished I had a ball or a large amount of meth so I could shoot it all up at once, or just go one bump after another until my eyes would roll back into my head and id be completely gone, dead... nothing could take the pain I felt deep within my heart... I was all alone coming off acid... on my knees in my living room at around 2-3am in the morning....tears running down my cheeks as I looked at the beautiful picture of my beautiful daughter, in pain... as a lost mother who wasn't a mother at all. who was completely lost, broken, who was mentally insane...

I remember crying and crying, crying out to whoever would listen... which now I realize gods always there, no one can hide from him,. I have tried and tried so many times to run and hide and avoid him completely.

I was on my knees crying out to god... I realize this today... I was crying out to him, and he answered...

I had an ancient cross that I had inherited from my grandma Marka hanging on the wall. I remember thinking about her, looking at that cross. You see she passed away when I was 20 year s old. I was too high to make it to her funeral... I never got to see her, because of my addiction. That cross meant a lot to me, especially since I just broke my mother's heart for not being there at all, for my daughter, for not being there for her when her mother had passed...

So many times I had broken her heart...

I stood up walked toward the =hallway coming off of acid, been up for days, slangin, stealing, livin in nothing but sin.

Walking over to the cross, Broken, with no soul...I was torn completely! I remember walking into my room, getting my outfit I was gonna wear..I had a counseling appointment.

I was too wasted to drive myself, so I had a buddy that had stopped by drive me. Although he had no license. He brought me there. I went to my counselors office, sat in the chair across from her.

We had the appointment for going into treatment. Honestly I was too far gone, no treatment place would help me... I went through the hour appointment pretty much regretting all that I refused later on in life...Maybe god would have chosen me to go to teen challenge then, but instead I refused her recommendations. left her office, went back to my car my buddy was waiting for me, so he could drive me back home. I was too burnt to drive myself. I was completely spiritually broken. My soul was Satan's, nothing could stop me... The treatment recommendations, the law, the love for my child, the love for myself... Meth takes complete control of one's mind... you belong to Satan if you put any substance into your body. and it then becomes an addiction... whenever I visualize a person's soul who's become dependent on meth, I visualize a Satan's taking your soul, by taking your breath away while he breathes slowly...as your cheeks start sinking in-your soul belongs to the devil, you no longer know or belong to god. you will keep doing all satanic and criminal bad things.

The day my house got raided, it was a hot summer day.. I had just got back from my counseling appointment, was coming down hard.

My co-defendant was awake. me him and my buddy that brought me to my appointment decided we needed a pick me up. we needed to go re up and pick up a bunch a dope to start back on our dealing.

So we were all 3 sitting at my kitchen table all the blinds are always down when you're a tweaker, due to being paranoid about the cops... Demons can come into your soul anytime if you do not know god, and especially when you're under the influence of methamphetamine.

We packed our pipe up, started smoking it...between the three of us.. at this time I had been shooting (IV use) up large amounts of dope continuously...I was approximately shooting a gram a shot.. My tolerance was so high by then...it was hard for me to get high anymore.. then you get the demonic thoughts of shooting more, more often different places..., pretty soon you're almost dead. while Satan just laughs at his work.

I wasn't getting high while us three were at my kitchen table. My codefendant had all of our dope on him which wasn't all that much. Just about a ball I would say.

All of a sudden we heard a huge BAM! BAM! Cop knock! Police were at the door. All I could then hear was "This is the Drug and Gang Task Force, open up the door..."

My codefendant ran for the bathroom, dumped the ball into the toilet, flushed the toilet...

As the task force had one of those bashing my front door in... with guns and about 10 officers and the head of the task force buschuck into my house...an officer had a gun up to my head, and "said" get down to the ground, while he forced me to my knees, I dropped completely down to the ground...At this time I was believing that all this was just a bad dream...I couldn't accept, care, feel, nor understand what was happening...I was so out of reality at this time my whole being was in complete shock...with a gun to my temples on the ground handcuffed, now thrown into my kitchen chair. This is the scripture that was broken mind, heart, and soul... was at this moment the day my house got raided...

This is what Satan does to his worshippers while there in his bondage...

* He was hidden like a bear or a lion waiting to attack me. He has dragged me off the path and torn me in pieces, leaving me helpless and devastachuck. He has drawn his bow and made me his target for his arrows.

He shot his arrows deep into my heart. My own people laugh at me. all day long they sing their mocking songs. He has filled me with bitterness and given a bitter cup of sorrow to drink. He has made me chew on gravel. He has rolled me in the dust.

Peace has been stripped away, and I have forgotten what prosperity is Lementations 3:4-17

I was in complete shock! I thought or wished I could just die right there.. I was nothing, I have lost everything...I've lost my soul, my beautiful daughter, my mom wouldn't let me have, I was selling, and using drugs... I then lost my place to live in.. My house got raided, Thank god my place was under my parents name...Along with my cars as well.

* the thought of my suffering and homelessness is bitter beyond words. I will never forget this awful time, as I grieve over my loss. Yet I still dare to hope when I remember this.

The faithful Love of the lord never ends! His mercies never cease!! Lementations 3:18--21

As I sat on my kitchen chair in tears, of shock, desperation, sadness and despair...

the lead at the Task Force was trying to scare me..Asking me where the rest of my stash was...Told him the truth "down the toilet"... my codefendant flushed it..That didn't go over good...He then escorted me upstairs, my codefendant was also arrested, handcuffed and thrown onto my couch in the living room. See the cops always separate everyone that's arrested and involved.

I hated cops to the max, today I have respect for them as long as they respect me also. As I sit here in Prison writing this to you!! I was brought upstairs to the room that we had built up there...

Thrown on the bed, told they had all these sale charges on me... I was looking at ten years...Trying to scare me, so I'd open my mouth...

I knew I was busted for sales, I confessed that I had sold drugs out of my place...Even when I was high I still had somewhat of a conscience,..Yet I was in denial, and shock of what just happened...

They went through everything, and when I say everything...They even read writings I wrote, notes, took numbers, took all cell phones, they found 1800 dollars, 5th degree possession due to paraphernalia...

Put both me, and my codefendant in the cop car...brought us to the jail... Booked us both on 5th degree possession took our scales, $, and paraphernalia...

They booked us in and all I could think about is how I wanted to just run...Escape reality completely!! I wanted to just die...Had all kinds of suicidal thoughts...I had given up a long time before the day my house got raided...I given up on myself and became suicidal with my drug use...I was shooting more and more after my parents said that I couldn't have my daughter because all the criminal activity I was doing, and they knew I was actively using. I wanted to just die while I was taking my mug shot for my 5th degree possession...The task force told me that they had all these sales charges on my...which I thought they didn't have nothing on me..They told me and my co defendant they would book us the release us...I was so messed up in shock, and gone... I just wanted out of this completely.

Looking back sober, they just wanted to watch me and my codefendant, cuz really they didn't find what they all wanted in my house...So they wanted to catch us for sure on something big on the next bust... I was still on probation from previous charges so my agent heard about the raid...Violated me on my 5th degree controlled substance charge I had taken the wrap for my ex (whose the father of my beautiful daughter) cuz I was so much in love with him... I had violated so many different times and I had told my agent I was done trying to follow her rules, that I just wanted to execute this sentence...

So my agent must have talked with the task force, so the leader of the task force came to my house, while my codefendant and mysclf started packing all my stuff up.. I was kicked out of my own house by my parents, bro, and myself..I didn't want to see or face reality of what had just happened or my family.

The officer arrested me out in the front of my house in front of all my neighbors...I asked him if I could call my mom...called her she answered...I said mom I'm going to jail now. I couldn't even cry, I was so spiritually drained, my heart aches...I had nothing, no one...I was suddenly in an emotion of being relieved. I felt some sort of peace within my soul. I remember thinking I can finally get rest...my soul was close to death...I was asleep right away after they put me into the back of the cop car...

* I lay down and slept, yet I woke up in safety, for the lord was watching over me..psalm 3:5

God saved my life...I had no idea at this time...all I know, now is that this was a "blessing in disguise"

at the time I thought this was the death of me. Little did I know this was the time I would become a new creation through Jesus Christ...

When I got to jail I remember the officers putting me into a holding cell...I was given 2 blankets, was still wearing my street clothes...I had a jail mattress laying on concrete floor...I instantly laid down...

*I was glad when they said unto me, let us go into the house of the lord.
Psalm 122:1

See, to me...every time I got locked up because of my bad choices..
while under the influence of meth or alcohol I was brought to jail...
which today threw my eyes is to god's blessing of protection...he has
saved my life so many times throughout my life of addiction on the
road to destruction...

They kept me in intake for about 3 days. I don't exactly remember
how long for sure because I was coming down so hard off of iv use
from meth... god was cleansing my soul and renewing my spirit...

Create in me a clean heart, o god and renew a right spirit
within me
PSALM51:10

I was brought to general population ...went to court the next day.
My agent showed up and she executed my sentence...so I had to sit 5
1/2 months in county, to finish off my year and a day sentence.

I remember feeling a huge burden being lifted from my shoulders.
I was spiritually, emotionally, and physically drained. still in
complete denial of what all that happened. Pretending it was all just
a nightmare...I went back to GP after my court date..I had my own
single cell and I cried myself to sleep...I slept for the next 2 weeks...I
got up to eat then went back to sleep...I was detoxing, coming down
off of meth..I was IV using pretty heavily when my house got raided...
Large amounts I would shoot up and stay up for days on end...I just
wanted to die. I have been running from all the things I've seen, been
through, and experienced. I was shaky, hungry, angry, lonely, tired...I
was coming down hard core...at this time when addicts come off of
drugs they can get aggitated, irritable, violent, crazy, hallucinate, go
through lots of highs and lows with their changes in mood. I was
experiencing all this at the same time.

I got into fights, got locked down, would cuss the officers out, hating everyone and everything around me. This is how I always would get while the demons were detoxing from my soul...It takes a total of 6 weeks to detox from meth...that is the drug is completely out of your body...your brain doesn't function, or become balanced until a year after you've been clean off meth. So, I was locked up once again...Broken and incomplete. I finally was detoxed completely from meth. this is where, then you come back to reality....life becomes more clear, and everything you did while you were high smacks you when you come back to society, and reality. I came back to reality going through everything that seems like one huge blur when your under the influence of meth...I was in complete shock and now had to think about without drugs.

As I sat my first couple of months in county, reflecting on what I had all done...I was completely broken. My family were so disappointed, and so worried about me. My mom's heart was broken once again, her thinking about what I was going to face...how long I would be going to prison for...I was in so much pain, sorrow, sadness, I couldn't deal with all this pain of facing reality...I was in such a low, I didn't talk about myself...wouldn't ask for anything...nothing! I was pretty much a walking zombie who was completely broken with no spirit. I was thankful my family still would talk to me,...My mom has my daughter. She knew when I had started using, selling drugs I wasn't in the right state of mind to have her. which she was right, I would always take care of her, yeti was under the influence of drugs, and would still be having people come and go at the end to pick up or drop off. I wasn't being a good mother to her at all. I thank god for my mother even today.

From jail I could still call and talk to my daughter daily. my mom would bring her up to see me every once in a while, her little soul would see her drug addict mommy threw glass. That would even break my heart even more...

See when your under the influence of meth and under Satan's control...you don't realize how bad you are effecting all the ones who love you...

Your conscience seems to be gone..The numbness, and control the meth takes over is so strong, that you don't even stop to think about the ripple effect of your drug use does to your family, children, society, to yourself, and how god is going to have you pay for all of the evil, selfish things we did while under the influence. I know this from experience, I've done a lot of time threw out my life of destruction with addiction. As I sit here in prison as I'm writing this to you.

God doesn't want to shame us or hurt us, or make us miserable... He just wants us to stop and think, feel, and realize where the path of our addictions or destructive behavior is leading us...

Down to the path to hell, unless you become saved and repent from your sins.

*Instead let us test and examine our ways. Let us turn back to the lord. let us lift our hearts and our hands to god in heaven and say" We have sinned and rebelled, and you have not forgiven us..."

So, I pray you open your heart for god, and ask him to forgive you of all your sins and you turn away from them and repent from them. It's all up to you . whatever path you chose is your decision.. God's path or the devils path. The choice is yours.

So, I was sitting in the jail executing my 5th degree controlled substance charge I had taken the wrap for the father of my child... After my house got raided, as I sat in the county I received all these arraignments to court, new court dates. w/ new pending charges.

Everything hit me all that I did on the streets came at me during those 5 1/2 months I had been serving.

I was shocked, didn't want to live anymore...

I couldn't believe this was actually happening to me...

Why would god let this happen to me? I generally a good person..I didn't try to hurt anyone, plus selling drugs...is minor compared to murder or being a sex offender...why was god punishing me with all these new charges. I was almost done finally with my 5th degree, I was going to be done with all this being stuck in the system.

Looking back now, I know that's exactly why god had everything I've ever done come down on me...I haven't learned and he wasn't giving up on me...

So, as I received all these new charges in the mail. I sat there alone in my cold cell in tears, crying out to god...Asking him why. Why do I have to do all this time...why did I have to always suffer because of my addictions?

Why did I have to go through all this pain that I've been through, throughout my life? What's the point of living...I thought my life was over...

Of course I could always roll on everyone...I was dealing with at the time...I never would! I told the cops "to do their own fucken job"! I wasn't nice at the time at all. This was where I had no one to turn too...I've always lost everything...I was a hott mess once again.

I told my mom about my new court dates...Which we knew something was coming up because of the raid...

She was ended up having a nervous breakdown....emotionally! Once again I broke her heart...I felt horrible, I felt as though my life was over.

I sat a couple more weeks and my mom just went and got a

$10,000 attorney...I never asked I just knew I was looking at a lot of time. They had two 2nd degree sales on me, I found out two of my close friends wore a wire on me...they must've got busted and were too scared to do their time...which even as a Christian today, I feel god has things happen to each and every one of us to discipline us, so we should take our own wrap...not snitch on anyone to get out of it.

I've forgiven my C.I's, for myself, and let god take care of the rest.

*think about it! Just as a parent disciplines a child, the LORD your god disciplines you for your own good.
Deuteronomy 8:5

We can't get out of our consequences no matter if we snitch or not, because god will make sure we all get ours.

I had several opportunities to snitch, honestly it crossed my mind for a second. My confidant and I referred to ourselves that we were always "riders"

So, as I sat waiting for my court date knowing accepting that I was going away to prison for a bit...Away from my beautiful daughter, my mom, my family...as tears rolled down my cheeks I sat in my single cell in the jail...I cried and cried!! asking god to forgive me!! I had given up on life...

*The lord hears the cries of the needy; he does not despise his imprisoned people
PSALM 69:33

See when we're locked up, when we're at our weakest moments... God has placed you there for a reason...To seek him, to cry- out to him during your weakest moments. For where we are weak he makes us strong.

While I executed my sentence on my 5th degree possession I got when I was 18..which I took the wrap for the father of my child... So he wouldn't go to prison. I look back at that, I was a "rider" then too...Just young, dumb, thought I was in love.

I was waiting for my court dates as I was executing on my 5th degree...My codefendant would come to visit me..Saying "you's my rider"...Really it didn't sound so good or cool anymore..God was coming down on me...or disciplining me to the fullest...see when my house got raided my co-defendant and myself both were selling together. The controlled buys were all on me...So, when I was locked up he was still out selling, and all that...Our dealers knew I was on my way to prison, so they had him make sure I was taken care of in there...they were all worried I would snitch on them. I would, or could never be a +rat" or a "snitch" like that..I just sucked it up and knew that, that's just part of the game, which I was deep into since the age of 15. At this time I was 22 going on 23.

So, I went to my PSI Court date with my $10,000 attorney... Then my attorney asked the judge if I could be released...with a court ordered to do treatment... I got released, I got into the treatment center . I graduated that treatment program, then was hoping and praying God wouldn't send me to prison...

My mom was so worried about me all the time...She would call my attorney asking about what was going to happen...Or if I was going to prison or not...He would tell her that yes...I was going to get sometime...Here I thought if I graduated treatment and kept my nose clean wouldn't have to go to prison.

I talked to my attorney at my last hearing before sentencing, and he had told me that the prosecuting attorney said they couldn't settle for me to go to treatment, and an extended Faith based program... Which was supposed to be at least a year or longer program.

So, after my attorney had told me that they would not budge on me staying at the faith based program (mainly because It wasn't a lock down facility). I couldn't believe what I was hearing. I kept thinking my attorney wasn't doing his job...My attorney also said that if I didn't plead guilty to the 3rd degree sales charges, they had a few other sales charges on me the task force had told my attorney... they were willing to let it go, as long as I plead guilty on the two 3rd degree sales charges and ran them together...I told my attorney I would plead guilty...But asked him to extend my sentencing court date as far out as possible.

In the mean time I was at the faith based program and all that had went down after I had found out I was for sure going to prison.

I had given up on god..Brought drugs into the faith based program. program corrupted the whole place with the devils dandruff and said "f it", I'm leaving this place and going on run.

I wanted to get as far as I could away from my prison sentence as possible...I didn't even want to think, feel, or deal with even accepting I had to go to prison...

I left the faith based program...was on the run now...Started seeing or sleeping with the father of my daughter.

I knew I had a warranty, so I couldn't stay with my parents, my house was being rented out now that I got it raided and was gonna be locked up for a while...

I loved the father of my child, but had fallen out of love with him after he slept with my brothers girlfriend. Which was my best friend at the time...This all took place when my house got raided.

Let me back up to while I was incarcerated in the jail. While I was feeling completely broken, spiritually, emotionally, and physically.

I started going to all the programs there..I knew I needed help. I also wanted to make my time go by faster.

So, if your locked up right now, just get involved in the programs they offer there.

So, I was incarcerated and attending all these programs I attended this Thursday night bible study! There was this beautiful older women.

At his time I was completely worried about going to prison, how long Id be away...Felt there was no way I could run or get away from this sentence.

*Don't worry about anything, Instead pray about everything, Tell god what you need and thank him for all he has done. Then you will experience god's peace, which exceeds anything we can understand. His peace will guard your HEARTS and minds as you live in Christ.
Jesus Philippians 4:6

As I walked into the Thursday night bible study, I could feel this presence of peace...not knowing then that I could feel God's presence.

I saw this women named carrie sat down beside (her), who along with the other inmates. IAs we did our bible study we read out of the portal prayers devotional book...started with a psalm that we looked up. Then another scripture, then we discussed it...At the end of the bible study she had asked if there was anyone who wanted to pray with her, and asked Jesus Christ to enter their heart...Right there I felt something deep within my soul...Telling me I needed this...I had know where else to turn. I was desperate for his help, anyone's help... carrie looked at me, saw my desire in my eyes...she came to me with open arms...Grabbing my hands..into hers...we prayed..I had tears running down my cheeks..Which I felt from the depths of my heart...

We asked Jesus Christ to come into my heart. I became saved October 18th 2007. I received the gift of salvation.

* He has creation us a new in Christ Jesus, so we can do the good things god has planned for us long ago.
Ephesians 2:10

After that Thursday night on October 18th 1007 (which is my oldest Brother's Birthday) I started reading the bible, praying, repenting from my sins daily, and saw the world from a different point of view. The way God's eyes see it...

He forgave all my sins and I became a Christian...

I really got into god's word, prayed to him, and began to have a personal relationship with him. as I went to treatment.I was serious to stay on god's path, and maintain my sobriety waiting to be sentenced on my 3rd degree sales.

I was doing fairly well in treatment the first month at treatment center, I would read, speak, ask God would want me too. Although all of us are sinners and fall short to the glory of god. I stayed to close to him, even when I got out for about a month.

Then I hooked up with this woman I was in jail with...And we got our girls together, then we both got to talking about dope and the lifestyle...Old times, seems as though we always remember the good times when we think about our past lives as we were actively using. Then thoughts turn into actions.

So, of course I called up my "hook up', or dealer and got some meth...shot it up then was up all night all spun out on meth...So, the devil got me in his trap once again through my addiction...I had given into Satan's temptation...as he worked through both of our weaknesses.

I had been doing pretty good in treatment, as a Christian staying in god's word, and living as a child of god. I strayed off god's path by using, God always forgives...All you have to do is ask.

Every time an addict relapses..It messes up your brain chemistry, which than corrupts the way you think act, feel. So I went back to group at treatment center. As I sat in group feeling guilty, sadness, and fear of my failure...at the end of the group the counselor tells the client (us) who has to take a Urinalysis and they have to take it that day by the end of the day or it is considered a positive UA.

I remember praying, and thinking, if I could just get away with this, I wouldn't use again. Well God knows everyone's heart.

*Guard your heart above all else, for it determines the course of your life

So, Thinking back god knew what my next though, action, and where my heart was. My counselor said to me "sky" we need a UA from you today...

I couldn't believe what I heard...I knew I would fail. So, I ended up telling the group I had relapsed. Then I was put on house arrest. I graduated the primary treatment, then was on house arrest. House arrest only lasted about a week.

I was waiting to be sentenced...I decided that following my probation was pointless, cause I knew I was going to prison for a while anyways...So, why even try to do good? or stay sober..II said "f it"...then went on the run...I was always good at running, numbing, and living the fast life...that's what I was good at...why not go back to what I was used to. My parole officer had us check in at a group meeting to let her know what we were doing...looking for a job etc...I stopped showing up for them.

So, my agent was looking for me..knew I was using and back to what I was used too.

I was hiding out at my parents house one day...after I was on the run...I was all spun out on dope...,y agent showed up at the door. my mom and I were the only ones there. my agent was at the front door the blinds over the front windows had been closed...my mom looked out the door window and seen my agent. she told me that my agent was at the door...I told her of course not to answer it!! As I ran to the kitchen to the closet and closed the door and hid, which then I wouldn't be in my agents view...

She continued to knock, ring the door bell...for about 20 minutes! I had just went on the run.

So, I decided then I needed to hide-out of a different destination...I had to run from the law, I needed to run from the pain I felt! I needed to numb the pain I felt...there was nothing I thought I could do except use dope to cope... so, I decided I would spend time with the father of my child, and my daughter..who I had left when I started using, selling, and when Satan had my mind, body, and spirit in his control...being under the influence of meth you are worshipping the devil and he has complete control over ones soul. So, I belonged to him...

I decided to stay with my ex (father of my child)...before I got locked up, and I was on the run..cops knew where my parents lived, and where mine and my brothers house was. plus I wanted to spend time with my "lil angel" before I had to go...I also was running from all my feelings, failures my prison sentence and from all the abuse I experienced and that I have done to others...

So, I was on the run staying at the father of my daughter. I had left the faith based program. and was actively using already at this time...I was spending time as a "family" with my daughter and the father of my child. We would spend quality time as a family together. See I wanted to have a family at this time, but wasn't happy...I didn't love myself,, I hated myself for all the things I had done, then my house got raided. I knew I wasn't in love with the father of my child. I just thought I didn't deserve any better. He controlled me, was verbally abusive, and obsessed with his young girlfriend. we had met when I was 17 years old and he was 36. we met through a drug deal, and he asked my for my number. I hated my life at home with my parents. I was sick of them telling me what to do, and the drunken crazy dysfunction. I experienced all my life. all I had ever done is run, run, run and never look back. Denying the truth or situations that had happened when I was younger with my dad's mental health and his alcoholism, my mom's alcoholism and the domestic violence and corruption I had lived my entire life.

All that was secret will eventually be brought into the open, and everything that is concealed will be brought to light and made known to all

Luke 8:17

Ever since I was a child. I was broken. God creates us and we are born "perfectly broken"/ Life's a test and a trust during our life...we than have a chance to live for god, or Satan. either we choose heaven or hell when we pass to the unseen world.

I have been running since I was a child, in a broken home. I then turned 15, and had this friend who's dad was condoning us to come to his place anytime and party. I was all for this, I would lie, manipulate my mom and I was there for weeks at a time. I started staying there even when my friend wasn't there. we all called my friend dad "dad" or Doctor chuck. I was 15 my dad was in jail and always craved a dad who would be there to guide me as a father should. I understand why he wasn't there because of his diagnosis as Bi-polar Manic Depression. He was also a veteran.

So, I trusted chuck as a "dad", he replaced my dad, cause he wasn't there for his kids.

We would party with our Dad or Dr. chuck. we experimented at 1ˢᵗ with alcohol, Marijuana, acid, ecstasy, shrooms, and then meth which was the beginning of my life under Satan's strong hold that at the age of 15 I had no idea what I was getting into.

I remember chuck shooting me up for the 1ˢᵗ time. He had asked me if I wanted to fly...of course I wanted to, I wanted to try all drugs once.

I got this really icky, scary, gut feeling throughout my entire body...just the way he so easily looked at me...and the way he asked me if I wanted to stick a needle in my arm. I was so scarred at that moment, but I trusted chuck, we all called him dad..he wouldn't let anything kill me or let anything bad happen to me if I got too high...

I figured it wouldn't hurt just to try this once...I knew what it had done to my brother and I knew I wouldn't let this take over me too. Plus it would be fun, and I love to party. I trusted chuck like a dad, and he always looked out for his girls...

As I was sitting on the edge of chuck's bed all strung out, looking into his eyes as he's sitting across the bed. Waiting for my response.

I know there had to have been a long silent pause after he offered to shoot me up with meth at the age of 15 for the first time.

I brushed all my thoughts of, gathers my thoughts..looked back to chuck and said, "yes" I wanted to try.

I can remember this so vividly like it just happened yesterday. I was 15, a star soccer player, was always happy, positive, very trusting of others, always accepting of others. I loved my friends at this time like they were family. I did everything I could for them...I would give them the clothes off my back if they needed. If I had $10, they'd get $5. Very loyal, kind, trustworthy, would take their place if they had got into trouble, I fought fights for them, always had their back through thick or thin...later I learned that a majority of my friends I considered close to family...their feelings or reliability wasn't mutual. They just got what they wanted from me taking my young naive soul for their free ride. Taking my kindness for weakness... I was completely heartbroken about this. The friends I met a chuck's place were at least 3-5 years older than me...

I stopped hanging with my school friends that I've known since kindergarten. I hurt a lot of them..

I just never understood me...My upbringing, my home life...Their lives parents, siblings weren't like mine. I felt as though I had to hide who I was, or how my personal life was at home just for their acceptance.

I pushed them all away, until they finally stopped trying.

How I could at, be, the real me...How I thought this life was supposed to be...

Alcohol, Drugs, Smoking, partying and having a blast was how I was born into life. I had started only to exist in my life. Which was the devils path down the downward spiral just like everyone else was. My parents, sister, 2 brothers, all my doped out older friends...

I loved not having to feel, care, or try at anything...

All the pain, sorrow, violence, abuse, was over, I could run so far, Get in deep, and just sit painlessly and got all drunk and geeked.

As Dr chuck (who we called Dad), got are the paraphernalia all together...sat and watched him get the spoon, cup with water, q-tips, meth, and syringe...

I remember watching him with my syringe...putting it in the cotton from a q-tip that was in the meth puddle in the spoon...

As chuck took the cap off my point put the needle to the cotton drew it back... to 35cc. He tapped the syringe 2-3 times as I watched little air bubbles disappear to the top to a thick controlled substance liquid in a syringe...

That was called "mine", in my friends dad's hands, who I called Dad...Dad finished with the procedure of the work that had to be done to shoot up meth, and to keep him in his high...and now to shoot me up to get high, and this as my 1st experience, 1st time that I had ever given a needle a thought I'd use on myself to get high...

I was screaming inside, knowing, telling myself not to give this a try. Today I know that was my holy spirit, my conscience, my innocence, the little girl that was locked up deep inside myself...

I never got the chance to be a free, spirited baby, toddler, little girl, pre teen, to 15 only the starting of maturing into a teenager, or young adult...

I also know the screaming, and in her turmoil; rejection I felt, heart and aching of my entire mind body, spirit and soul...This was god speaking

It was god, and his assigned angel that was my guardian angel, they were speaking, nudging, demanding, that I would or could find the strength to say "no" and all their prayers they had been praying for me, to me... I now know what and why I had that inner spiritual experience and feeling... when offered to use iv meth. I wish I would know what I know now. I had no spiritual religion, or a belief in god... never was thought of, talked about or cared to hear or learn about...

So chuck, was looking at me... Touching my lower arm..bringing my arm closer toward him...and his syringe he made especially for his "girl'

He squeezed my arm close by my shoulder... Pressuring my veins to be popping out to make them more visible...

My heart was pounding, I started sweating, my inside was still screaming.

As chuck found the perfect vein, I looked away, as I felt the needle break through my outer layer of my skin, then to my virgin vein...

It really did sting, and I felt the pain!! From the mutilation I allowed to be done to me...

I had my eyes shut, my face turned the opposite way...My hands clenched in fists, my teeth clenched tight, along with a tight jaw...

Coping mentally, physically with the sting, and pain, and the fear as a scarred little girl, wishing she, as a little girl, told them how she truly felt...

I was so afraid, but I always wanted to be accepted, and at age 15 especially running with the older crowd. I knew I did what they did to be able to get there respect and acceptance.

I wish I would've known that god was right there, waiting for me to just grab his hand, and he would protect me from Satan's trap. My new life on Meth.

Gods Courage

The lord is my light and my salvation so why should I be afraid? Don't be afraid, for I am with you. Don't be discouraged for I am your god. I will strengthen you and help you. I will hold you up with my victorious hand

Isaiah 41:10

As the meth ran through my veins, I felt my body temperature race my heart pound in my chest...

My body completely relaxed...I was high on chuck's bed in a haze...I wasn't thinking I was just laying there, my eyes fluttering, my vision was blurred my eyes crossing... and I don't remember what I did at this time...the devil got me..that day..he worked through chuck taking me to..Satan's hell.

At this time my dad was incarcerated, and it was just my mom and I at home. She totally trusted chuck. She was starting to really worry about me. She knew I was drinking alcohol and smoking cigarettes at this time.

I remember at this frame, my mom knew I was doing or using something, because I wasn't the same.

She would let me stay at chuck's house overnight. Only because she thought I was always staying with chuck's daughter. She was hardly ever there...

The night chuck shot me up with dope she wanted me at home the night before. I didn't call to check in with her and she couldn't get a hold of me.

I'm not sure how long I was missing, or not in contact with my mom.

I was rebelling against my mom, and lying to her about my use, and everything else that went with it.

Finally after 4-5 days passed by I woke up in the laundry room across chuck's room...

I was so drained, mentally, physically, and emotionally.

I couldn't exactly remember what I was or had been doing.

I rolled over to my side realizing I was naked, looking to the side of me there chuck laid...Next to me...I covered myself up scarred, confused, and at shame. In shock as tears went down my face... I wrapped a blanket around,myself and ran to the bathroom.

I gathered my emotions the best I could. Wandered down the hall to Chuck's room looking in a panic for my clothes. I found them next to his bed.

Got dressed, called my mom, and had her pick me up.

I was crying, she could tell!

My mom had been worried sick for me. She was angry, in a panic and on her way to come get me.

I sat. On the front step in a daze...No thought...I felt sick to my stomach, and threw out my entire body. I was in shock.

My mom pulled up, came flying to me from her car grabbing my shoulder and tugging, and pulling me toward her car,, screaming, yelling loud at me...I seen the neighbors across the park staring toward our way. I didn't even care...all I could think about was chuck and I.. laying unclothed. chuck was next to me!! and he as unclothed!! Why were we both without clothes!!!

I was without an answer to my questions...I was speechless, and so unstable...I really didn't feel like me...

My mom and I drove to our house. She lectured, cried, and vented all I had put her through those last 3-5 days...

I wasn't hearing or even able to comprehend a word she was saying...My mom than grabbed my shoulder and looked into my eyes...she could see I was in shock, silent, in a fog and on something.

Mom, let me alone and I slept, and had memories, events, of what had went on.

chuck shot me up with meth and Roofie so he could have his way with me...

Made me do things, took pictures, had sexual intercourse...with me. raped and sexually abused me for 3-4 days until I woke up.

I stayed in bed, withdrawing, and trying to heal from the rape and abuse.

My mom knew I was using...she didn't know what happened. She grounded me which I was believed didn't want to see him or anyone...

When I was sleeping, chuck called my House for me...mom told me. She thought it was odd I didn't react or call him back.

My entire body ached I got the sweats, shakes, and chills. I had track marks on my arms...my body was craving...I fought those urges for as long as I could.

I then gave up and knew I needed more...

after about a week of repressing, denying, and pretending the abuse didn't happen and it was just a bad dream.

I went back to my crew and chuck (dads) house.

I felt like I was dying... I had to use to get by...After he IV used the needle on me, I needed that, I would no longer get high snort or smoking it any more. My urges were intense without meth... and if I didn't iv use I was just chasing... that fix...chuck made a full Blown Demon Addict Monster! After the abuse, and all the pain, suffer, I went through...I then would shoot more and more dope..."numbing and forgetting all Temporarily

I was a freshman in high school.

The police contacted me, and wanted me to know details they busted chuck. He had been doing this to young girls for years.

I wouldn't testify due to being ashamed etc..he was sentenced to 5 years.

I was brought to adolescent rehab. I went in with the attitude I could get more hook ups. I got out was clean maybe a month.

I then met my 1st daughters Father. He was a dealer.

I got pregnant, then went to prison.

While he was gone I met Ben He was another know violent drug dealer. At this time I was drug dealing myself in St Cloud area...He was from Monticello. Which is where I'd pick my dope up for way cheaper, then went back to cloud to flip the dope and make money and support my habit.

Ben and I fell in love. we used,uit sold and tweaked together. we were in the honeymoon stage.

I remember the first beating I experienced from Ben. He had no car, no house. we stayed at his mom's place. I had a apartment at where I am from.

We were driving or I was and he put the car (my car) in park when I was going 65-70 mph. My whole transmission was done...He smacked me in my mouth, my car was smoking. I cried but punched him back... Then he got out the car, came to my side and grabbed me out threw me down and started kicking me in my ribs over and over again.

Meanwhile the police got called.

My car was totaled and I just got physically handled as though I was man vs. man.

The cops came and seen I was bleeding from my mouth and nose.. I could barely breathe due to my chest, and stomach were all bruised up...

The cop asked my name...I told him my sister's name. I lied and said we got into an accident and took all the blame.

The cop offered to give us a ride, we accepted. we had tim tow my car (a friend of Ben's)to his lot there it sat.

The relationship got worse and escalated from there.

I was his...I was an object. I belonged to him. We sold, and used lots of meth together.

During my relationship with Ben, he raped me numerous times. Kidnapped me when I ended it...He came and found me..He sold my car, Money drugs, and myself all the time. He ruined me...I was never the same after being with him.

After all the sexual verbal and physical abuse I've went through... all I wanted and needed to keep going to be able to cope with all these nightmares I survived and lived through... I would use and use and use...Due to wanting to repress, mask any memories, feelings or flashbacks of these nightmares of abuses.

So, I really got deep into selling large amounts.

I ended up getting busted. Sales charges 2nd and 3rd degree sales. They raided my house, I flushed all the dope I had in my possession...

I got sentenced to 36 months in prison...I never flipped, sold, or ran anymore drugs since my raid, and bust.

Prison was rough. 2 1/2 years away from it all, especially my oldest was literally torture.

I went to prison in 2008-2010

I remember like it was yesterday.

It was my 2nd oldest brothers Birthday. I went to the birthday party.

While I was in Prison, God was present and I grew a genuine strong relationship with him. he set me free and I felt it. I no longer wanted meth and that lifestyle... I wanted a family, to get married in my near future.

At my brother's party I met the love of my life...He had blue eyes and broad shoulders with strong muscular arms. He was trim, about 5'9"

He was having some beers, but never got deep in the dope lifestyle. He had no children, never been married. I met the man of my dreams.

We fell head over heels on each other. Life as a couple was great... While he figured out I relapsed and started using. He has been through so much with me because of my addiction.

I always tried to hide it from him, but he always figured me out...I would lie and lie and lie just to hide how bad I had got. He always believed in me though. He never once gave up on me or us.

three years into our relationship we found out we were pregnant. I was so gone in my addiction I used while being pregnant with my son. He was the savior of my life..I believe I'd be dead if I hadn't got pregnant. I got sober because of my son and daughter!!!

I stayed sober for my kids for almost 4 years. Life was good, I was struggling with mental health severe depression at this time. My father was diagnosed with stage 4 lung cancer.

I was diagnosed with manic depression while I was sober for 2 years. While in cognitive thinking treatment during my prison stay. My father was also manic depressant along with my grandma. I never accepted my diagnosis due to trauma from childhood from my father's manic episodes. lots of domestic abuse towards my mom and older brother.

In the almost 4 years I was clean after my son was born, Jim and I got married in 2014. One of the best memories of my life. Jim was the one for me. I knew it from the day I met him. He has saved my life along with God many times through my life of trauma, and addiction.

After we married, we planned our baby girl Addison. My father seen Jim propose to me. He never seen or walked me down the aisle on our wedding day. He passed 2 months before our wedding. Broke my heart. We miss him so much.

Sometimes, I believe God brought him home...So, another can live like me, and my mom...

After my Father's passing we had started drinking.

We got married and had our beautiful wedding on September 6th 2014...Now we've been married going on 4 years. Love him with all my heart...He's my rock, my all...

I believe I didn't have god in my life through all trials and tribulations I've survived through, I'd be dead and gone away...still using.

I wake up in the morning every day, do my prayer and meditation. I do devotions and reading meditations.

I believe my recovery has been given through a gift from god... There's been so many times through my life where I should've been dead!! By the grace of god I'm still here. I've overcome my Meth addiction. the devil no longer has my soul.

You can overcome anything with prayer and god...I pray this book helps your mind body and spirit. No matter how bad you think it is... or how bad you've had it, you can do it...

Printed in the United States
By Bookmasters